Brett F

Sloth and the Art of Self-deprecation

Indigo Dreams Publishing

First Edition: Sloth and the Art of Self-deprecation
First published in Great Britain in 2018 by:
Indigo Dreams Publishing
24, Forest Houses
Cookworthy Moor
Halwill
Beaworthy
Devon
EX21 5UU

www.indigodreams.co.uk

ISBN 978-1-910834-85-5

British Library Cataloguing in Publication Data. A CIP record for this book can be obtained from the British Library.

Designed and typeset in Palatino Linotype by Indigo Dreams.
Cover design by Ronnie Goodyer at Indigo Dreams.
Cover image by Mark Sparx. Twitter @sparxart.

Printed and bound in Great Britain by 4edge Ltd.
Papers used by Indigo Dreams are recyclable products made from wood grown in sustainable forests following the guidance of the Forest Stewardship Council.

These poems are dedicated to all the sloths in this life –
numbers of toes being irrelevant

Acknowledgements

Thanks are due to the editors of the following publications where some of these poems (or versions of them) first appeared: Algebra of Owls, Amaryllis, Clear Poetry, The High Window, Hinterland, Ink, Swear & Tears, Laldy, Main Street Rag, More Raw Material (anthology, Lucifer Press), Outburst, Picaroon, Poetry Spotlight, Riggwelter, The Saranac Review.

Thanks of biblical proportions are also due to Phil Robertson, my ever constant anchor, and Holly Magill for their support in these poems and outside of them, and for the many conversations that inspired Sloth's narrative here. My very different love to you both.

Also by Brett Evans:

The Devil's Tattoo, IDP, 2015

CONTENTS

PREFACE

Sloth on the Rocks

Sloth's urine defiles
his canopy, far above
the dirt's industry

where ants and beetles
busy themselves. Sloth could rise
should he dare to fall.

Philosophies and Maladies

Now, there's a man.
He knows there's no heaven to reach up to
and squeeze the fucking sac, burst its balls of purpose.
So he wastes his life, in control of that alone.
Doesn't shroud himself in Jesus, accost strangers,
spout the sermon on the mount;
interpret texts to suit self-interest,
obsessions. He dedicates himself to truancy,
not philosophy, economics, politics;
of the people, for the people, fuck the people.
Wallowed in debauchery, he comforts his arse
on a cushioned barstool.

But that boy there, stood still on the bridge,
excesses driven beyond volition,
ghouls sprinting the ginnels
of his brain; he'll have lolloped years, naked,
through electrocuting hail, laughing like a bonobo,
then from the bridge, drop, as he does now, to slide
along the railway lines both his blues and reds.

Sloth

Sloth is in a tree of his own;
two-thirds his weight lolls in his hairy gut.
He will only descend to shit and bury his turds,
easy prey for those who condescend, resenting
Sloth's days of decadence where no muscle is flexed
or put to work – he knows the wages of sin
is what we all get paid. Not quite as somnolent
as they'd like, it occurs to Sloth he couldn't give a toss
for slurs by those who cannot see the irony
in looking up to him, frustrated by his apathy,
green in their envy. And in his coat of algae,
time for a nap, Sloth suspects
he may merely have dreamt them.

Downloads

Over one thousand indecent images of children,
it reads. And the print begins to blur
as I've my own images to process: his face
(familiar to me over pint glass and newspaper)
lit blue by the screen – hairless skin, thin limbs
flashing across his spectacles – and any emotion
it may betray; guilt, the one I search for,
my gut depressed by an ambiguous weight.

Faces of other friends, then; scarred by slashes
of sunlight through the windows of the bar.
Some expressionless, awaiting the full
magnitude to load; bellies, troubled seas of beer.
One or two spout mob mentality, recollections
fabricated to substantiate the case against
the accused. Strange to miss his company
though no longer desiring it.

It is later that they parade before me –
the children; not what abominable acts were committed,
not what he must have got off on, just fragile
body after fragile body of broken children
circle the bed. I do not believe that he lay
a finger on any. That is no absolution;
let him sit in front of parents, stare intently into the monitors
of their eyes and assure them that a childhood can be retrieved.

I attempt to log off but my server is not responding.

My Mother, the Barmaid, Never Said There'd Be Nights Like This

It's nights like this you expect that heart attack,
as pipes announce the lungs of the house collapsed.
The body shakes and sweats and sweats and shits,
trumping Christ – your skidded Turin sheets.
Busy as the arse has been, the brain reflects
on friends, drink, individual lovers, sex,
the need for skin on skin, a tattooed shoulder.
Your soaked breast tightens, heartbeats may go no further.
Your 'fuck-it list' complete but now you're dead,
eternity won't bring one hour of Bessie Smith,
Sweet Emma Barrett, or Tampa Red.

Sloth on the Cross

Sloth is dredged from torpidity
by a strange breed intent on banging on
about a man dying for sins. Sloth asks
if we all aren't, and in his wooziness
swears he hears *himself* a sin;
rich, he thinks, from unsolicited
slumber-wreckers.

Welcome to his sins; Sloth hopes
that they won't wash his sleep away
yet does his best to remain alert, endure
their noon-time story. Sloth's lazy thinking,
between belly and ball scratches,
concludes they do disservice
to the back-stabber who did himself in.
Sloth reasons the back-stabber, money-grabber,
grafted for Big Chief Slumber-Wrecker
unawares; part of His, decidedly wacky, plan.
No, a dastardly cad, and Sloth's too tired to argue that.

Sloth's asked about the ending of the world
and remembers a time when he thought it had;
hours before this unholy interruption. And now wishes
it would again. They drone on and Sloth daydreams
he's permanently fixed to a timber rest
before being elevated skyward – seems idyllic,
but not for shy and simple Sloth;
all that adoration
and misinterpretation.

Hot Club de France

They're making love: the Gypsy's and the Jew's
six-string guitar and hot-jazz violin.
First notes are intimate as taste, then carnal
acceleration to a frenzied bacchanal;
illicit lovers charged by a medicine
of passion; taboo jazzing up their blues.

The attentive stroke of bow across the strings,
its confidence and sultry melody
arouses responses of cocky, staccato licks:
hammer-ons, pull-offs, virtuoso tricks.
Both push their dangerous tune, ferocity
born of their obsessive imaginings.

Poor companions for me, the Gypsy's and the Jew's
six-string guitar and hot-jazz violin,
who incessantly speak of lust, seduction, sex
in red-hot tones over one's frets, both necks.
On nights I cannot kiss her freckled skin
I hear their *appel direct*, can read their *billets doux*.

Positively Shit Street – Rhyl to Venus
for Mark 'Sparx' Hughes

Trousers off and wrapped round our heads,
worthless diamonds pitting pavement
and bare legs on a five mile homeward stagger,
pissed and potless, Mark slurs Should shee Venush
ish mornin'.

Daybreak caravanned to the moon,
our offbeat feet felt light years from home.
Beneath trousered heads, coats flapped like bats
and laughs howled the Tom Waits wannabes back
into doorways, their proud fag ends dying.

When the sky took to grey, we halted in Pensarn's salt air;
legs in revolt, stumbling shoulder to shoulder.
I stood with this man I love, trousers on head,
glaring through cigarette smoke at the vast cosmos above –
goggling Venusians wondering what fucking planet we were on.

Sloth on Fine Dining

Sloth's favoured position for eating
is legs above head – not his own legs, of course –
and being the slothiest of sloths he'll lunch
at the laziest of leisure; a real underachiever.

Accomplishing more than fool-sloths,
whose tongues are prized as mere limbs
obtaining tasteless leaves beyond their can't be arsed
reach, Sloth revels in the rainforest-wet of his reward;

lapping up all he needs to nourish fruitless days.
And don't be duped to think that starburst effect
cunted down thighs, up spine, out to tips of digits,
or any echoed cries from the canopy above enough

to lull Sloth into some nuzzled slumber. He's more
than awake, face already tucked into his second course.

Talking Martinis with Eddie Condon

Of course no olive, Eddie, Jesus:
gin and vermouth (stirred) – a little water
from the discarded ice. And one yourself, Eddie.
We've no use for embellishments, you and I.
Steady with the vermouth, more gin.
The way jazz is going they'll be mixing
vodka in martinis next.
Imagine that, Eddie – a flavourless cocktail.

Cheers, Ed. That hits the spot.
Speaking of jazz, no beboppers
in your club I notice – flattening their fifths,
leaving us to drink ours. Reactionaries or revivalists,
labels belong only on bottles or shellac discs. And only then
when well informed. Sure, I'll have another.
Mencken said it was the one Yank invention
as perfect as the sonnet.

Oh, let's not start on poetry: too much garnish
before we even reach the olives. More gin, less vermouth.

The Martini as Big as The Ritz

A mixing glass in which you could launch the Ark,
enough ice to reassure the polar bear,
so little vermouth to cause France to revolt,
and stir as vigorously to cause civil war.
That aromatic wine strain down the sink;
you want this guillotine-sharp. Enough gin
to make Hogarth sketch again,
Hemingway shudder, Roosevelt
and Churchill to shoulder each other,
Bogart to falter through a Faulkner script,
F. Scott Fitzgerald to admit that he's pissed –
this night could never be tender.
Think The Raft of the Medusa when stirring again;
strain cold spirit, discard ice like the hopes of the pole
and bask in the bullshit that heroes only need gin
in frosted glass that shows no reflections,
and the art of self-deprecation.

Sloth on the Dawn Chorus

Sloth is not of the belief
that even music lovers wake up singing.
The birds may be lamenting the early light
and no lie in. Some screech, some hoot,
some with shoulders back look to seize
the fucking day and all who have disturbed it.
Sloth can't consider it a chorus
if they are all intent on different tunes.
He feels his late noon yawns
and farts much more symphonic.

Sloth among Clarinets and Brass

Sloth is approached as vocalist
by The Wafting Duvet Jazz Band:
no one's as laid back as Sloth
since Leon Redbone, they say.
And that Sloth has an affinity
for the blues. Sloth claws his greenness,
questions the colour-blindness
of his instrumentalist admirers, yet wallows
in temptation: to be lifted by a force of sound
alone and the irony to croon Sporting Life.
His lids begin to droop;
Sweet-Georgia-Brown-dreams, Sloth.

Realising his rudeness in not yet replying –
the founder members stand open-mouthed
at the idle ball scratches, uncontrollable cock twitches –
Sloth is suddenly struck by the hostage situation
of being placed between cornet player and trombonist;
such up-close noise pollution. And the concept
of exercising one's voice is alien to simple
Sloth, who can not help but feel pain and pity
for The Wafting Duvet Jazz Band, him now slipped
through their fingers. A yawn in perfect b-flat
is the first note that drifts Sloth
off to Frenchmen Street for the afternoon or week.

Wild Bill's Celestial Jazz
for Wild Bill Davison 1906-1989

> '...no harder-driving, or more masculine, cornet in the entire business.' – Eddie Condon

Born in Defiance (that's geographical as well as literal)
wailing b-flat into a life of lust and vice

that your appetites craved until the grave –
a bolshie enough bastard to take such a calling further.

And should such a place exist and you had entered there
via some loophole or celestial, administrative balls-up

(or maybe God called you to teach Joshua a thing or two)
then I'd fear for His angels: any with cocks

would be seduced into joining you on a frenzied bacchanal;
any in a frock best watch her tits and crotch.

No doubt angels are inclined to forgive. And so they should;
their brass would only sound sweeter fuelled by such ferocity.

And all the blessèd tapping their feet as your thunder
blew over your home. Wild Bill, they'd say. Defiant in death.

Big Women and Men of Imagination

The man of imagination needs to know he has mapped
territory worthy of report, a skinny isthmus
is only ever of slight importance; his preferred
expedition is of the vaster plains. Zaftig sculptures
whose beauty was appreciated in a more
civilised age reaffirms he has not been duped
by fickle fashions, and that where women
are concerned, the maxim *less is more* proves
a fallacy. The man of imagination drops anchor
at port between sizable thighs.
Without leaving the covers he wants to feel
he has circumnavigated the globe,
held the world in both hands.

Sloth on Sociability

(and his New Year's exercise regime)

Sloth considers himself gregarious.
His comfort zone a cushioned barstool
beneath the overhanging mahogany, bottles,
optics. Often surrounded by others,
Sloth is no slouch – it is no idle thing
being selective in whom to sup
with and who to grumblecunt fuck off.
Yet Sloth loves no-one more than those who pour
and serve his drinks – despite their over exerting
his loose-change work. But changes
need to be made and Sloth regrets
beneficial opportunities missed.
So should Sloth decide to morph
into bark and leaf, mattress
or couch, to snooze a calendar day
or two away, even Jehovah's,
Mormons, Conservative candidates,
cold callers ignoring the No Cold Callers sign
are more than welcome. Diatribes
to be exercised can only burn
off a fuck-load of calories.

Bull

On the piss with Daedalus
in the snug of The Bull, no less.
He drained his pint of Speckled Hen
and bade farewell to all his friends,
"It's no place for my son."

All jaws dropped (it *was* his round),
an awkward hush, then speech was found.
"You cannot think of leaving us,
you know we all love Icarus
and drinking's just begun."

"I want to see him carve a life,
not waste it in this den of vice.
He has a head for dizzy heights,
no stomach for our drunken fights –
so boozers he shall shun."

This genius bought one last shout,
we drank his health and he was out.
Followed by the hobbledehoy
whom we had cherished since a boy,
for families we had none.

Icarus' searing slide
blues guitar could charm the tides,
bring tears to Willie McTell's eyes,
and at the bar we all took pride
in the house of unrising bums.

Of course he joined the 27s –
we'd taught the boy there was no heaven
to reach and that the Devil's music
soared on scotch. But he abused it.
Don't we feel such cunts?

Poor Daedalus returned a wreck.
The Bull refused to stock the meths
that he required to speed up death.
We didn't drink more, did not drink less –
refused to cut out fun.

So first we toasted Daedalus,
waxed lyrical on Icarus,
two clever dicks now lost to us –
we have but one life therefore must
live low, avoid the sun.

Sloth Pitches his Reality TV Show

Sloth shits once a week.
He reasons there has to be a series in that.
And if the focus be that one turd, Sloth
insists there's no space for those two
Geordie gobshites or that egotistical
Pied Piper for pouting teens twat
whose haircut not even the Amazonian
rain could run off.

Monday to Friday, Sloth will snooze and scratch,
narration will describe his unique ecosystem
to the disinterest of viewers in the build up to Saturday's
equivalent of entertainment's colonoscopy
when Sloth is sure he can cash in on the phone votes
– in or out?

Animal

It was wild; refused to be tamed.
Let loose to do its own thing, it tore up
the park. People shook heads, made remarks;
but there's beauty in an unbroken mustang,
elegance in the tiger that leaps to devour you.

Breaking the pond water, it lapped
and guzzled a frantic swim, churned
comfort zones of small fry and pike,
scrambled the bank, passed out in the shade;
revived, it lunged, began again.

Now muzzled, from living seven years
for every one, it is resigned to a cage
out back, out of sight. Some nights I hear
its low snarl, as a dog in disturbed sleep;

an involuntary curl of the lip,
my head gives a swift twitch –
and I thought I'd run the bastard
until his heart had burst.

Sloth in Vogue

The pre-teen in the chair looks at his barber's
reflection then points to a style from the gallery –
Gimme a Sloth; the lice that hatched from *Lardy Balls,*
the instrumental hit single dubbed with snores and scratches.

Kids are impressionable but not easily fooled,
though no one saw through the book signing gimmick:
Sloth being too sloth to even be present,
none suspected that stint in the Priory pre-booked

six months before any signs of addiction. Of course
not even PR could have seen the need for the return
stretch upon Sloth being released to a world of three foot six,
green headed, snot faced clones.

Salt

When they find his body – The Fat in Black,
forever attired for his own funeral – the man
himself will be long gone. As he always was.
Interred in the second-hand wingback chair
with torn upholstery – decorative Spartans
cutting loose with their xiphoi
desperate to free themselves of this dead weight –
unfinished gin to his left, read and unread
books to the right, headphones skew-whiff,
the brain will have ceased its silent singing
of The Streets of Laredo. The only traces of living
being the salt stains on his shirt.

Sloth Adored

Sloth's soiled dressing gown drapes open,
his hairy chest a bowling green gone to the dogs.
Would-be beauties of groupies hang on his every slur
and reality TV status. All tramp stamps and Groucho
eyebrows on Oompa Loompa tan: Miss Yeovil
and Miss Chepstow compare their shellacs
to Sloth's maniclaws whilst he moans
in satisfaction of Miss Merthyr Tydfil's massage.
Sloth ponders a sequel series:
Mmm, Sloth Gets Off.
He idly recalls that tale of the Christ
and can only assume that this is what it's like
to have so many disciples, believers.
Yet the bulge in Sloth's loincloth leaves no room
for misinterpretation.

A Final Note

Dig up Louis Armstrong the second I die.
Johnny Dodds too; reheat the Hot Fives and Sevens,
they've had their cold rest – I've a humble request:
Potato Head Blues or Struttin' With Some Barbeque,

a swinging sugar rush to send me off.
As mature and complex as an Islay malt:
that syncopated poet's stop-time slant rhymes –
robust in tone, that lingering smoky finish.

Indulgent of me to expect feet to tap
the crematorium’s floor to music so many funerals old
and me in no state to appreciate its crackerjack abandonment.
These tunes would not be hummed later, haunting a mourner's lips.

No. Respects shall be paid by passing tangible notes
over a much more familiar bar.

Sloth's Panto Season

'It's behind you!' they yell, and Sloth knows
they roar the truth – it's all behind him.
Celebrity had been and gone, the fickle
public no longer cared on what day
of the week he shat.
The white-dressing-gowned portraits
in *Hello!* soiled by a keen-eyed reader
writing in to highlight that infamous
upside-down-Africa urine stain.
The much derided, ghost-written memoir
stripped and recycled; 'Pulped Fiction'
the tabloids mocked, and never gave weight
to publishing Sloth's quiet
'Oh no it isn't.'

Sloth and the Snake
for the Standing Rock Sioux

Sloth farts himself awake,
groans indescribably – deprived
of sleep as he already is; bickering
neighbours, yelps and yawps have stolen
Sloth's beloved canopy of lullabies.
And Sloth knows he's too simple
but this morning, even he picks
up on disturbances. Sloth's shoulders
stiffen momentarily as strength
is mustered to reflect on the beauty
of all he can see, and tune into protest songs
beyond water cannon and rubber bullets.
The black snake is about to slide
across the wide Missouri – far away,
that rolling river – and it's not
the ever mournful leaves
that spill onto Sloth's once carefree cheeks.
Energy enough to chide *Too simple*
for this world, battling his eyelids
knowing dreamcatchers grasp
less than he does, Sloth feels fresh;
snatches the closest branch
as if it were a lance.

Indigo Dreams Publishing Ltd
24, Forest Houses
Cookworthy Moor
Halwill
Beaworthy
Devon
EX21 5UU
www.indigodreams.co.uk